KOMODO DRAGONS

THE REPTILE DISCOVERY LIBRARY

Louise Martin

Rourke Enterprises, Inc.
Vero Beach, Florida 32964

Library of Congress Cataloging-in-Publication Data

Martin, Louise, 1955-
  Komodo dragons.

    p. cm — (The Reptile discovery library)
    Includes index.
    Summary: Describes the physical characteristics,
habitat, and behavior of the largest
monitor lizard in the world.
    1. Komodo dragon—Juvenile literature. [1. Komodo dragon]
I. Title.
II. Series: Martin, Louise, 1955-
Reptile discovery library.
QL666.L29M37 1989   597.95-dc   88-29729 CIP AC
ISBN 0-86592-574-7

TABLE OF CONTENTS

KOMODO DRAGONS

Komodo dragons *(Varanus komodiensis)* are the largest of the family of monitor lizards. Komodo dragons look just like the magical, fairy tale dragons we read about in books. The only difference is they don't breathe fire! These strange creatures were named after the island of Komodo in Indonesia, where they were discovered.

Komodo dragons are big and powerful

HOW THEY LOOK

Komodo dragons are huge lizards. They can be as big as ten feet long and weigh 300 pounds. Komodo dragons are covered in a tough, reddish-gray scaly skin. Young dragons have yellow speckles. Komodo dragons have pale yellow tongues. These tongues are long and ribbonlike, and they constantly flick in and out of the komodo dragon's mouth. Komodo dragons' legs are thick and strong. They have razor sharp claws.

This young komodo dragon still has his yellow speckles

WHERE THEY LIVE

Komodo dragons can be found only on four islands in Indonesia. The islands are Komodo, Flores, Padar, and Rintja. Komodo dragons are usually found in the forests and grasslands of these islands. They dig burrows in the hillsides where they sleep at night. The burrows are only four or five feet deep, so the dragons have to bend in two to fit inside.

At night komodo dragons sleep in burrows like this

WHAT THEY EAT

Komodo dragons are **carnivorous** and will eat any kind of animal, dead or alive. When young, they feed on insects. As they grow, their **prey** includes small **mammals**, birds, goats, wild pigs, deer, and even water buffalo. Komodo dragons eat both fresh meat and **carrion**, the flesh of dead animals.

Komodo dragons eat all kinds of meat

One bite can kill . . .

Komodo dragons bask in the sun to raise their body temperature

HOW THEY EAT

Komodo dragons' teeth are perfect for tearing flesh. They are sharp and daggerlike, with a **serrated** edge that saws through the toughest meat. If komodo dragons break their teeth, new ones will grow. Komodo dragons are very greedy. They sometimes eat so much they cannot move afterwards. Scientists saw one dragon eat a sixty-pound wild boar in seventeen minutes.

Komodo dragons are large enough to kill and eat goats

THEIR SENSES

Komodo dragons have a highly developed sense of smell. The dragons' flickering tongues pick up scents and feed them into special sense organs. Called Jacobson's organs, these are located in the roof of the komodo dragons' mouths. The Jacobson's organs **analyze** the scents and send information to the brain. The komodo dragon then knows if it has scented food.

Komodo dragons use their long tongues to gather information

THEIR DEFENSES

Komodo dragons have no enemies in the islands where they live. This could be one reason why they have grown so large. Komodo dragons do not have sophisticated defenses. Like some of the other lizards, they use their tails as weapons. These tails are strong and powerful and can knock down smaller animals with one blow. One bite could also severely injure another animal.

Komodo dragons sometimes fight each other for food

BABY KOMODO DRAGONS

Baby komodo dragons hatch from eggs that their mothers have laid in holes in the ground. The eggs are four inches long. When the baby dragons hatch, they measure twelve to eighteen inches. For the first year, baby komodo dragons live in the trees. They do not dare to come down to the ground — the adults might eat them. They only risk coming down from the trees when they are three feet long.

Young dragons do not feed with older ones until they are large enough to protect themselves

KOMODO DRAGONS AND PEOPLE

Since 1912, nobody has been allowed to kill komodo dragons. The dragons fear people and run away when they smell them nearby. If they are threatened, or perhaps hungry, komodo dragons will bite. They are not poisonous, but their bite can kill. It carries disease from the carrion they feed on, and there is no known **antidote**.

GLOSSARY

analyze (AN a lyze) — to find out what something is by studying it carefully

antidote (ANT e dote) — a medicine used to stop poison from working

carnivorous (car NIV uh rus) — meat-eating

carrion (KARE eon) — the flesh of dead animals

mammals (MAM uls) — animals that suckle their young

prey (PRAY) — an animal hunted by another for food

serrated (SAIR ay ted) — notched, like the edge of a saw

INDEX